I0012046

Contents

APPLE VISION PRO

:

UNLEASHING THE POWER OF SPATIAL COMPUTING.

Apple Vision Pro is Apple's augmented and virtual reality headgear, a product that has been in development for more than a decade. Vision Pro is the company's first debut into a new product category since the 2015 Apple Watch, with the device introduced at WWDC 2023 in June. Apple plans to accept pre-orders for the Vision Pro starting on January 19 at 5:00 a.m. Pacific Time, with a launch to follow on February 2.

While the Apple Vision Pro is certainly a headset, Apple does not use that word when referring to it. Instead, Apple calls it a spatial computer because of its potential to blend digital content with the actual world. Apple claims to the Vision Pro as the first spatial computing device.

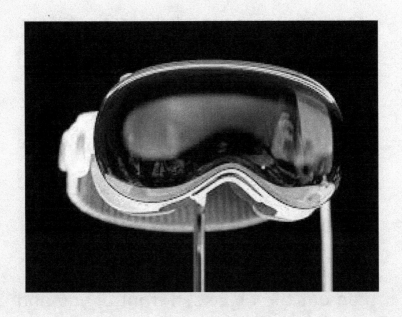

Apple Vision Pro is a headset that combines augmented reality and virtual reality. It shows augmented reality content on top of the real environment and also provides immersive virtual content. However, it's important to mention that the headset does not allow you to see through it. All that you observe is in a digital format. Apple utilizes cameras to create a digital image that combines virtual elements with the actual world, without making your surroundings disappear. These cameras map out the objects in front of you and translate them into augmented reality material.

During a virtual reality encounter, Apple disables those cameras and creates the illusion of complete isolation from the surrounding environment, enabling you to concentrate entirely on the content displayed on the screens of the headset. This transition between the "actual" and the "engaging" can be managed using an on-device Digital Crown.

In terms of design, Apple Vision Pro is similar to a pair of ski goggles, with a single piece of laminated glass for the front that seamlessly connects to an aluminum alloy frame. A gentle, snug Light Seal is magnetically attached to the frame and molds to your face to prevent light from entering.

Two Audio Straps with integrated speakers are located on the sides of the headset, providing Spatial Audio that combines the sound from the headset with the sounds in the surrounding environment. The Audio Straps link to a 3D knitted headband that holds the Vision Pro in place. Apple designed it to be breathable, cushiony, and stretchy for comfort, and a Fit Dial ensures the headset fits tight against your head. Additionally, there is a two-strap design that evenly distributes the weight between the back and top of the head. Apple intends to provide Light Seals and headbands in various sizes, and these parts can be exchanged.

Inside the frame, there are two micro-OLED displays that deliver over 4K resolution to each eye for a total of 23 million pixels. There's also an external display called EyeSight that projects an image of your eyes so people can tell whether you're using the headset in an immersive mode or if you can see what's going on around you. For glasses wearers, there are special prescription Zeiss Optical Inserts that may be connected magnetically to the headset's lenses.

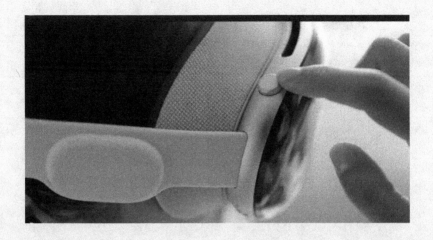

There are no controllers for Apple Vision Pro, with the headset instead operated by eye tracking, hand gestures, and voice instructions. An app can be navigated to and highlighted by gazing at it and then opened with a tap of the fingers. Scrolling is done with a simple flick of the fingertips.

More than a dozen cameras and sensors in Apple Vision Pro map out the world around you, keeping track of your hand and eye movements. Optic ID, which scans your iris using infrared lights and cameras, is used for authentication. Each person has a unique iris pattern, and Optic ID is analogous to Face ID and Touch ID. It can be used for unlocking the device, making purchases, and as a password replacement.

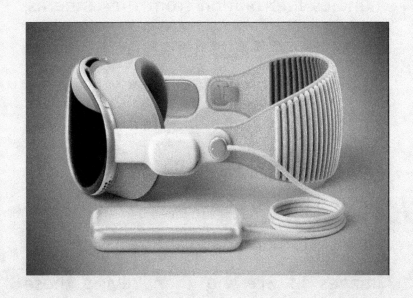

There are two Apple silicon chips inside Vision Pro, including the same M2 chip that's in the Mac and a new R1 chip. The M2 processor runs visionOS, conducts computer vision algorithms, and provides graphics, while the R1 chip handles information from the cameras, sensors, and microphones.

Apple Vision Pro can take 3D photographs and videos using a built-in camera that's powered by tapping on the top button of the gadget. Apple says that customers may capture videos and images in 3D and then revisit those memories like never before. Vision Pro will also show existing photographs and movies at huge dimensions, making them more immersive. Note that when you are recording video, Vision Pro makes it evident that recording is happening with an animation on the external display.

Due to weight concerns, Apple did not incorporate a battery in Apple Vision Pro. Instead, it can be powered by a braided wire that is coupled to a battery pack worn at the hip or plugged into an adaptor. The battery pack gives up to 2.5 hours of battery life on a single charge.

With Apple Vision Pro, content is shown in the environment around you. You can position programs and windows in mid-air, rearranging them as you see fit, with multiple windows available. Apple says there's an "infinite canvas" to work with. Apps can be displayed in the actual environment that you're in so you can be present with what's going on around you, or you can utilize a more immersive view that shuts out the world and puts content on a virtual background called an Environment.

A visionOS operating system runs on Apple Vision Pro, and it includes a dedicated App Store with programs built exclusively for the device, but it is also able to run iPhone and iPad apps. You can connect the Vision Pro to a Mac, with the headset functioning as a display for the Mac. It works with Bluetooth accessories for text input and control, or you can use virtual typing or speech for text.

There is a main Home View that features all of your favorite Apple apps including Mail, Messages, Music, Safari, Photos, and more, with your data linked through iCloud. The UI is similar to the iPhone interface, however you may open apps and arrange them digitally. Apple is updating its primary apps for visionOS and has created APIs for developers, plus Apple is releasing Vision Pro test kits to developers for app testing. Apple Vision Pro delivers an immersive experience for entertainment like TV and movies, and the Apple TV app will offer more than 150 3D titles at launch. Content can be stretched to feel like it's in your own personal theater, complete with spatial audio.

FaceTime has been redesigned for Vision Pro. People on the call are shown in huge tiles to the headset wearer, while the headset wearer is shown as an accurate digital reconstruction utilizing their Digital persona. With FaceTime, Vision Pro users may collaborate on documents with colleagues or share apps with others, and spatial audio makes it apparent who is speaking.

The Cinema Environment allows you to watch shows and movies at the frame rate and aspect ratio set by the designer, or you may utilize a nature-themed Environment to make the screen feel 100 feet wide. Apple created Apple Immersive Videos that are 180-degree 3D 8K recordings that place consumers right inside the action, plus streaming services like Apple TV+ and Disney+ are available on Vision Pro. As for gaming, Vision Pro supports Apple

Arcade, with 100 iPad titles to be available at launch. Games can be played with Bluetooth gaming controllers that link to the headset.

Apple Vision Pro is priced starting at $3,499 and it is expected to launch on February 2, 2024. It will only be available in the United States when it releases, with Apple accepting orders both online and in retail shops.

How to Buy

The Apple Vision Pro is expected to launch on Friday, February 2, with Apple accepting pre-orders starting on Friday, January 19 at 5:00 a.m. Pacific Time. Demos will be offered starting on February 2 for individuals who wish to try out the headset before making a purchase.

The Vision Pro will be available in U.S. retail outlets and for purchase from the U.S. online store. Apple does not plan to deploy it in other countries until later in 2024, although Apple analyst Ming-Chi Kuo has said that it will expand to new nations before WWDC 2024, which takes place in June.

Pricing starts at $3,500 for 256GB of storage space. The pre-order process will need a Face ID scan to assist buyers identify the optimal Light Seal and head band fit.

Apple is expected to sell out of the Vision Pro at launch. The company is creating between 60,000 and 80,000 pieces, and despite the expensive price, the restricted availability and demand among core fans will certainly force available supplies to be drained shortly. Those looking for a Vision Pro on launch day should plan to pre-order right now.

Zeiss reading lenses for the Vision Pro cost an extra $99, while bespoke prescription lens inserts will be priced at $149. A valid unexpired prescription from a U.S. eye care provider will need to be submitted after purchase in order to acquire custom prescription lens inserts.

What's in the Box

The Vision Pro ships with two bands, the Solo Knit Band and the Dual Loop Band. It also comes with a Light Seal, two Light

Seal Cushions in different sizes, an Apple Vision Pro Cover for when the headset is not in use, a Polishing Cloth, a battery, a USB-C charging cable, and a USB-C power converter.

How It Works

Because Apple Vision Pro is a "mixed reality" headset, it can show content from both augmented and virtual reality.

But unlike augmented reality glasses, it is made to completely cover your eyes and obscure everything around you.

Apple's augmented reality feature makes use of both internal and external cameras. With the use of see-through glasses, you are able to view an accurate representation of your real-world surroundings even though you are not actually looking around you since the cameras are able to map the space around you and display the real world back to you.

With this feature, Apple can display 3D windows, objects, and content in your real space. Alternatively, you can switch off the cameras to create a completely virtual environment. Apple is emphasizing how the Vision Pro headset enables users to work, consume content, play games, communicate, and engage in other "anywhere" activities.

Design

Although Apple does not call its wearable "spatial computing" device Design Vision Pro a headset, that is precisely what it is. The Apple Vision Pro is a head-mounted virtual/augmented reality headgear that resembles Meta Quest or the PlayStation VR.

Design wise, the Vision Pro looks similar to a pair of ski goggles, albeit high-end goggles. It features a laminated glass front, which Apple says was "three-dimensionally formed." The glass is attached to a curved aluminum alloy frame that wraps around the face. As of now, the headset is only available in silver with matching gray Light Seals and

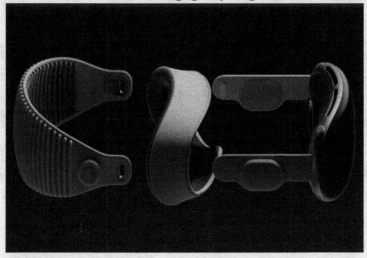

band

The Light Seal, which Apple sells in a variety of shapes and sizes to match various facial shapes, is magnetically attached to the frame and rests on the face. For the headset to function properly and to filter out light, the Light Seal must fit snugly. Apple made the Light Seal bendable in order to accommodate different face shapes. A poorly fitted Light Seal lets light seep in and makes the Vision Pro display hazy.

Two audio straps with speakers that provide spatial audio are located at the side of the headset. The headset is fastened to the back of the head by a 3D braided fabric Solo Knit Band, which is connected to the audio straps via an

A dial that may be adjusted to tighten it up for a personalized fit.

Because the primary braided headband is detachable, wearers will be able to switch it out for one that fits them better in terms of size or, should Apple decide to release more designs in the future, style.

To let customers to select the optimal fit, the Vision Pro comes with two bands: the previously mentioned Solo Knit Band, which fits around the back of the head, and a Dual Loop Band, which goes over the top of the head and around the back of the head for weight distribution. Unlike the Solo Knit Band, the Dual Loop Band is constructed of a different braided fiber and features a two-strap construction.

Early adopters of the Vision Pro have reported that the headset is hefty, therefore they find the Dual Loop Band to be more comfortable. The device's weight has come up in several reviews, along with the fact that wearing it might be uncomfortable.

Physical controls include a top button that doubles as a camera button to take 3D "spatial" recordings and pictures, and a Digital Crown that modifies your "immersion" level and shows you approximately what's around you through "Environments."

The braided wire that powers the headset can be attached to the opening on the left side of the headset. The round charging puck rotates to firmly click into the headset, but it doesn't appear like the charging puck for an Apple Watch.

The charging cord fastens to a power adapter that is plugged into the wall or an external battery pack that is worn around the waist.

Display

Apple claims that the 23 million pixels available on the two specially designed micro-OLED panels in the Apple Vision Pro are "more pixels than a 4K TV." Although the headset displays have a 90Hz refresh rate by default, 24 frames per second movies can activate a 96Hz refresh rate.

Although the displays' size has been described as that of a postage stamp, the hardware specifications are yet unknown.

Additionally, there is an exterior "EyeSight" display that allows others in the room to see the wearer's eyes. People can use this function to determine if the wearer of the headset is in a completely immersive virtual reality mode or a less immersive augmented reality mode.

An internal camera that records the wearer's eye movements provides the eye display that is displayed on the external display. Additionally, it can notify others when you use the external camera to shoot video.

Lens Inserts

Zeiss Optical inserts with their prescription can be ordered by Apple Vision Pro users who wear glasses. Zeiss lenses cost $149 for readers or $99 for a custom prescription. The displays within the headgear will be magnetically attached to the optics.

Cameras and Sensors

Twelve cameras and five sensors are used in Apple Vision Pro to map the surrounding area and track hand movements.

Two of the cameras transmit more than

a billion pixels per second to the display to depict the real world around the wearer when using augmented reality mode, while the others are used for Real-time 3D mapping, hand tracking, and head tracking.

In low light, infrared flood illuminators improve hand tracking, while LiDAR depth sensors let you locate and measure things in the room.

The headset has four infrared cameras and LED lights within it for eye tracking. The Vision Pro can determine the precise location of the wearer's gaze for navigational reasons thanks to its technology.

Getting Around

The Vision Pro is not equipped with any physical controls. Voice-activated instructions, hand gestures, and eye movements are used for navigation. For instance, in visionOS, you can use a simple hand motion to open an app by highlighting an element, such as an app icon, with your eyes.

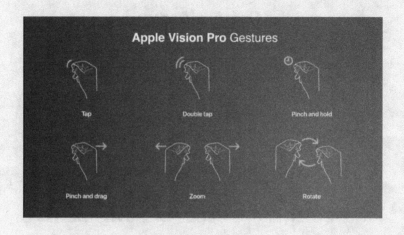

Apple Vision Pro Gestures

Tap — Double tap — Pinch and hold

Pinch and drag — Zoom — Rotate

Although they are primarily intended to be used with an Apple Arcade game connection and with a Mac, Bluetooth keyboards, mice, trackpads, and game controllers can be linked to Vision Pro as an additional navigation method.

Videos taken from the visionOS program are used to demonstrate eye and gesture-based navigation. Apple guides customers through the process of examining a system component and tapping it with their fingertips. Even with hands comfortably resting in laps, hand movements can be detected by the headset.

Optic ID

Optic ID is a security feature of the Vision Pro that makes use of its infrared cameras and LED lights. Similar to Touch ID or Face ID, Optic ID use iris scanning rather than fingerprint or face scanning.

The headset can identify each individual's distinct iris pattern to protect sensitive data stored on it. Similar to Face ID, Optic ID can be used as an alternative to passwords for purchases, device unlocking, and authentication.

3D Camera

With the Vision Pro, users may examine 3D photographs and videos taken with Apple's outside camera in three dimensions. Apple claims that because of the "incredible depth" that is available, using them is similar to reliving an experience in person.

When recording is enabled, the camera clearly indicates so that it is impossible to record video covertly using the headset.

The spatial video capability on the Vision Pro has been tested by a number of media representatives, and reviews have said that it's so realistic that it's almost unsettling.It fosters intimacy in a way that two-dimensional photographs cannot, according to Wall Street Journal's Joanna Stern, while CNET's Scott Stein noted that the movies are simple to produce with the iPhone 15 Pro models and appear "compellingly realistic."

Audio

The speakers are integrated into the straps that are fastened to the frame, and there are speakers on either side of the headset. The speakers include dual-driver audio pods adjacent to each ear, and they can adjust the sound to fit the acoustics of the room by analyzing its characteristics.

There are six microphones for voice commands, video calls, and phone conversations in addition to the speakers' capabilities for spatial audio, which creates an immersive surround sound experience.

The USB-C AirPods Pro, which were released in September 2023, provide 20-bit, 48 kHz lossless music with extremely low latency when linked to the Apple Vision Pro, providing users with an enhanced listening experience.

Connectivity

The 2.4GHz and 5GHz bands are used by Wi-Fi 6, which is compatible with the Vision Pro. The speedier Wi-Fi 6E specification, which is compatible with the 6GHz band, is not supported by it.

RAM and processors

There are two chips that power the Apple Vision Pro. The M2 microprocessor, which debuted with the 2022 MacBook Air, serves as the primary CPU. Its duties include supplying graphical content, processing content, executing computer vision algorithms, and operating the visionOS operating system. An 8-core CPU and a 10-core GPU are features of the M2 chip found in the Vision Pro.

Every piece of data originating from the cameras, sensors, and microphones is handled by a second R1 chip. Apple claims that in just 12 milliseconds, images may be streamed to the panels.

provide a "virtually lag-free" perspective of the surroundings.

The Vision Pro's internal thermal system regulates heat and enhances performance by silently pushing air through the headset.

Dynamic random access memory, or DRAM, specifically engineered to accommodate the R1 input processing processor, will be utilized by the Vision Pro headset. Apple will receive 1-gigabit low latency DRAM chips from SK Hynix, which feature more input and output pins to reduce delays. There will be 16GB of RAM in the headset.

Storage

Although Apple is anticipated to release variants with up to 1TB of storage, the entry-level Vision Pro comes with 256GB of storage.

Battery Life

The Vision Pro has a two and a half hour battery life when using an external power pack; 2.5 hours is the recommended duration for watching 2D material. Apple claims that the Vision Pro has a two-hour battery life for everyday use.

Though there is a single battery pack included in the gadget, they may be changed out for more power on the move. The Vision Pro has a full day's battery life when plugged into a power adapter.

visionOS

The operating system called visionOS, which Apple created especially for the headset, is used by Apple Vision Pro. The "infinite canvas" feature of visionOS allows app windows to move anywhere in the area around the user.

Apps such as FaceTime, Messages, Safari, and more have been rebuilt by Apple to function in a 3D environment. In addition, the headgear is compatible with the whole library of iPhone and iPad apps. Apps for the iPhone and iPad can be used on the virtual canvas, but they are not optimized for 3D.

With Apple TV+ and other apps, you can stream movies and TV episodes that can be resized to appear to be "100 feet wide." Apple has developed unique immersive 3D content specifically for visionOS, and it also has its own App Store.

Because it can be operated entirely without the need for physical controls—using only hand gestures and the eyes—visionOS is referred to be the first spatial operating system.

Macintosh Integration

A Mac can be used with visionOS as a display. It functions as a massive external display for Mac content, and linked keyboards, mice, and trackpads provide users with familiar capabilities.

Future iterations of the AR/VR headset may have accessibility settings intended to assist those with visual impairments and eye disorders.

Apple's Medical Examination

The Vision Pro may one day be utilized for mental health diagnosis and treatment. Apple has conducted tests on the Vision Pro, tracking a user's facial expressions to identify various conditions such as sadness, anxiety, tension, and post-traumatic stress disorder (PTSD).

Apple thinks that it can measure a person's "affect," a psychology word that describes how a person expresses emotions, using pupil dilation, eye tracking, and external cameras. If an issue is identified, the Vision Pro may play appropriate visuals and audio to help the wearer feel better.

www.ingramcontent.com/pod-product-compliance
Lightning Source LLC
LaVergne TN
LVHW051615050326
832903LV00033B/4513